OLIVIA GOES TO THE ZOO

AN ADVENTURE WITH THE VOWEL O

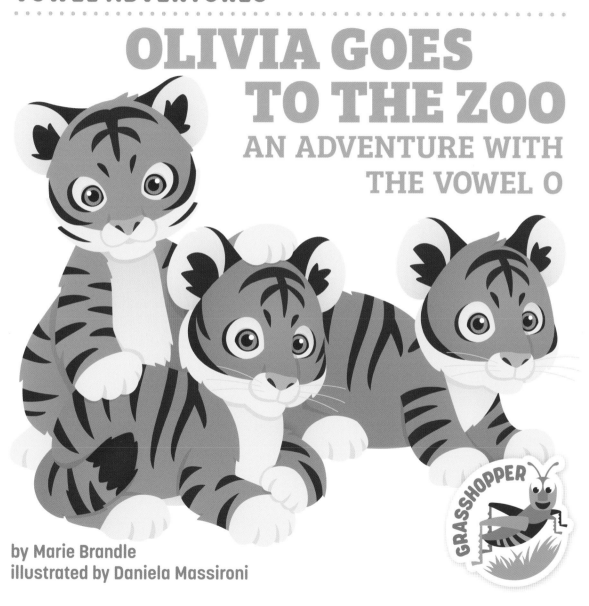

by Marie Brandle
illustrated by Daniela Massironi

GRASSHOPPER

Tools for Parents & Teachers

Grasshopper Books enhance imagination and introduce the earliest readers to fiction with fun storylines and illustrations. The easy-to-read text supports early reading experiences with repetitive sentence patterns and sight words.

Before Reading

- Look at the cover illustration. What do readers see? What do they think the book will be about?

- Look at the picture glossary together. Sound out the words. Ask readers to identify the first letter of each vocabulary word.

Read the Book

- "Walk" through the book, reading to or along with the reader. Point to the illustrations as you read.

After Reading

- Review the picture glossary again. Ask readers to locate the words in the text.

- Ask the reader: What does a short 'o' sound like? What does a long 'o' sound like? Which words did you see in the book with these sounds? What other words do you know that have these sounds?

Grasshopper Books are published by Jump!
5357 Penn Avenue South
Minneapolis, MN 55419
www.jumplibrary.com

Library of Congress Cataloging-in-Publication Data

Names: Brandle, Marie, 1989- author.
Massironi, Daniela, illustrator.
Title: Olivia goes to the zoo: an adventure with the vowel o / by Marie Brandle; illustrated by Daniela Massironi.
Description: Minneapolis, MN: Jump!, Inc., [2022]
Series: Vowel adventures
Includes reading tips and supplementary back matter.
Audience: Ages 5-7.
Identifiers: LCCN 2021002207 (print)
LCCN 2021002208 (ebook)
ISBN 9781636902463 (hardcover)
ISBN 9781636902470 (paperback)
ISBN 9781636902487 (ebook)
Subjects: LCSH: Readers (Primary)
Zoos—Juvenile fiction.
Classification: LCC PE1119.2 .B736 2022 (print)
LCC PE1119.2 (ebook)
DDC 428.6/2—dc23
LC record available at https://lccn.loc.gov/2021002207
LC ebook record available at https://lccn.loc.gov/2021002208

Editor: Eliza Leahy
Direction and Layout: Anna Peterson
Illustrator: Daniela Massironi

Printed in the United States of America at Corporate Graphics in North Mankato, Minnesota.

Table of Contents

Around the Zoo

"Ready for the zoo?" Mom asks.

Olivia nods. "Of course!" she says. She hops out of the car.

Olivia spots gorillas.
One pounds its chest.

"Wow!" Olivia shouts.

Olivia points. "Look!" she shouts. "A sloth!"

The sloth moves slowly. It has two toes.

A kangaroo hops.
Its pouch holds a joey!

8

"Oh, boy!" Olivia says. "A fox!"

It hops over a log.

9

Next, Olivia spots lions.

One chomps on a bone.
Another roars!

"So loud!" shouts Olivia.

Olivia and her mom go on.

An owl swoops down
from above.

It hoots.

The zoo is closing soon.

"Could we come
back tomorrow?"
Olivia wonders.

"Possibly!" Mom says.

Let's Review Vowel O!

Point to the words with the short 'o' sound you saw in the book.
Point to the words with the long 'o' sound.

hops　　　**bone**　　　**toes**　　　**log**　　　**sloth**　　　**over**

Picture Glossary

chomps
Chews or bites
something.

joey
A baby kangaroo.

pounds
Hits heavily.

swoops
Flies down through
the air suddenly.